UNDERSTAND HOW TO DRAW DS8

Drawing Light and Shade

Peter Caldwell

SEARCH PRESS

Introduction

To me light and shade are important and dramatic aspects of drawing and I would even say that the proper and effective use of these techniques makes the difference between a good drawing and a mediocre rendering of the subject. This applies just as much to the great masters of painting, as to enthusiastic amateurs striving to improve their technique.

Before mankind learned to write, drawing and speech were the only means of communication. With a little perseverance the ability to draw is in all of us, even if the results are not as good as we would like. Whatever your level of competence, drawing is a pleasant, relaxing experience that will encourage you to look at your surroundings more closely and to understand them better.

Sketching is fun and you should always carry a small sketchbook around with you. Through sketching you can study what is around you and use it as reference for future pictures. Some of my smaller sketches are like shorthand notes; I am constantly recording unusual patterns which catch my eye, or fleeting tricks of the light that I want to capture.

Just as handwriting distinguishes one person's script from another, similarly it is very rare to find two artists with the same style. We might start off trying to copy or imitate a particular artist's technique, but as time goes by and progress is made, our own characteristics begin to creep in. So we in turn develop a style and technique of our own.

Learning to draw is rather like learning to drive a car. There are three stages: first you need to be shown the basic equipment; then you have to go through the sometimes agonising process of constant practice, while getting accustomed to which piece of equipment does what; finally there is a gradual realisation that you are drawing without thinking about the method, and consequently you are much more relaxed and the experience is more enjoyable.

The analogy with handwriting is appropriate. How often do we think about our style of writing, having acquired the necessary ability? Seldom, if at all. We just concentrate on the message, or if we are drawing on the subject to be drawn.

Shadows add form and depth to the objects in this simple pen and ink drawing.

Equipment

Drawing and sketching requires very little inexpensive equipment. Nearly everything you need can be carried around in a pocket or small holdall, except for the paper of course. I have made a tough, waterproof wooden sketching folder for myself, with a carrying handle (see overleaf) and this is my most valuable piece of equipment. You must be prepared for any sort of weather when you go out sketching.

There is a seemingly endless variety of papers available these days, to suit every medium. As you experiment and practice you will be able to sort out which you feel happiest with. Drawing paper ranges from smooth to rough. Smooth takes line easily, whereas rougher papers are better for tone drawing. Some examples are given on the following page.

Looking through foreground trees' shadows greatly adds to the picture's charm and depth.

Cartridge paper is the most popular paper for drawing; it is available in a variety of surfaces – smooth, semi-smooth and rough.

Ingres paper has a soft, furry surface ideal for pastel drawings and is made in a variety of light colours – grey, pink, blue, buff, etc.

Bristol board is a smooth, hard white board used for fine pen work; it is available in various thicknesses.

Sketchbooks are compiled using nearly all of the above papers and are an essential piece of equipment for the artist.

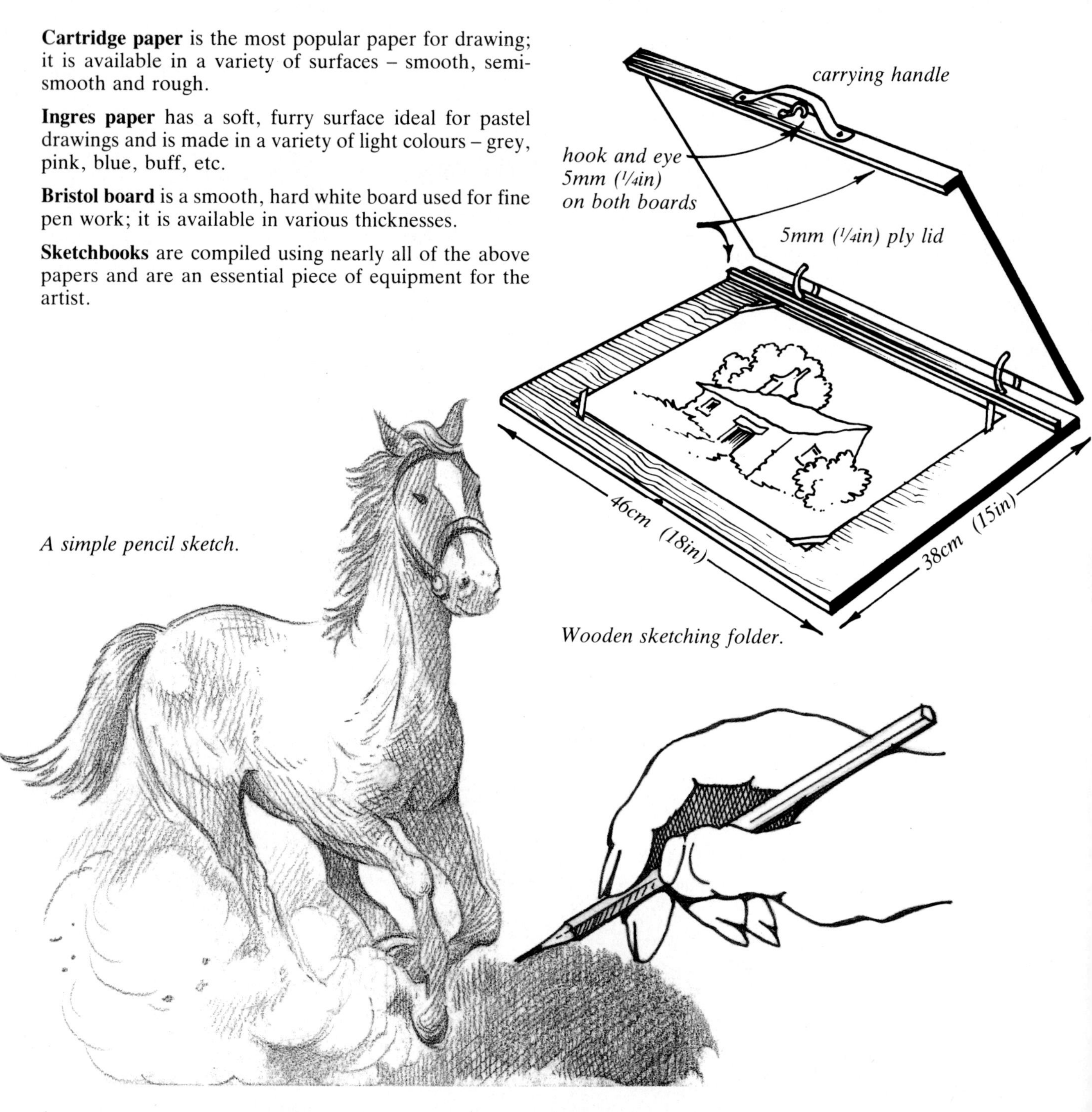

Wooden sketching folder.

A simple pencil sketch.

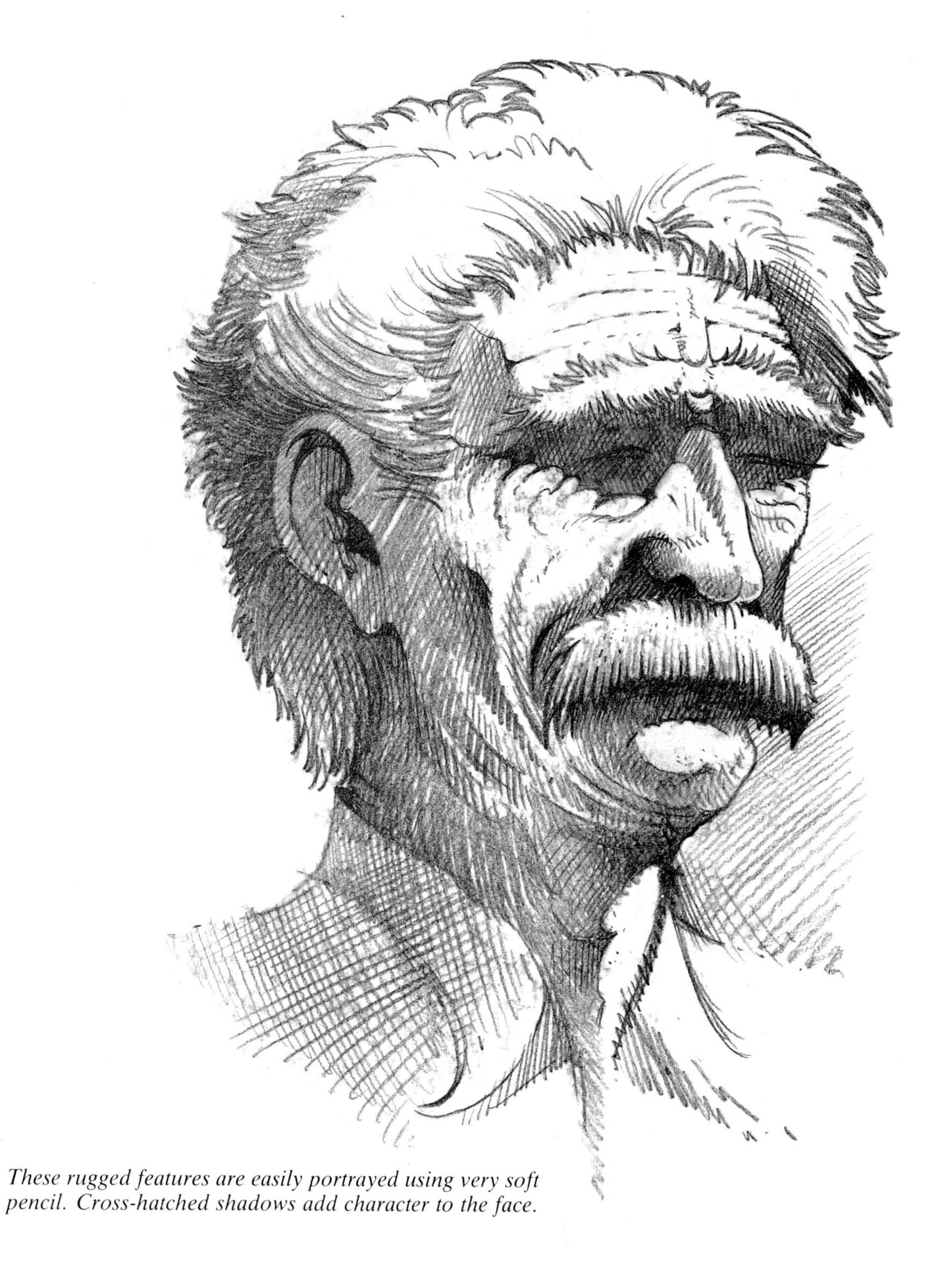

These rugged features are easily portrayed using very soft pencil. Cross-hatched shadows add character to the face.

Pencils are graded according to hardness and softness – 'H' to '6H' (the hardest), 'HB', then 'B' to '6B' (the softest). I prefer the 'B' grades for my sketches and drawings. The pencil will do everything, from a small rough sketch to a bigger more elaborate finished drawing. The side of the lead is as pleasant to draw with as the point. I recommend that you keep two pencils next to your drawing, one for outlines and detail and the other for shading. If you only use one pencil you will forever be sharpening the point.

Charcoal stick is excellent for large, bold sketches, but it is not good for detail. A charcoal pencil can be used for this. You must be careful not to smudge the drawing. Fixative must be sprayed over the final drawing to 'fix' it.

Wax crayons are quite soft and do not smudge easily. They are excellent for large, bold sketches and are available in a wide range of colours. Oil pastels, marker pencils, chinagraph and lithographic chalks have a similar quality and feel to wax crayons and can be used on almost any type of surface.

Conté crayons give a very rich, soft texture. By using the side edge in alternatively hard and soft sweeping strokes a variety of interesting effects can be achieved.

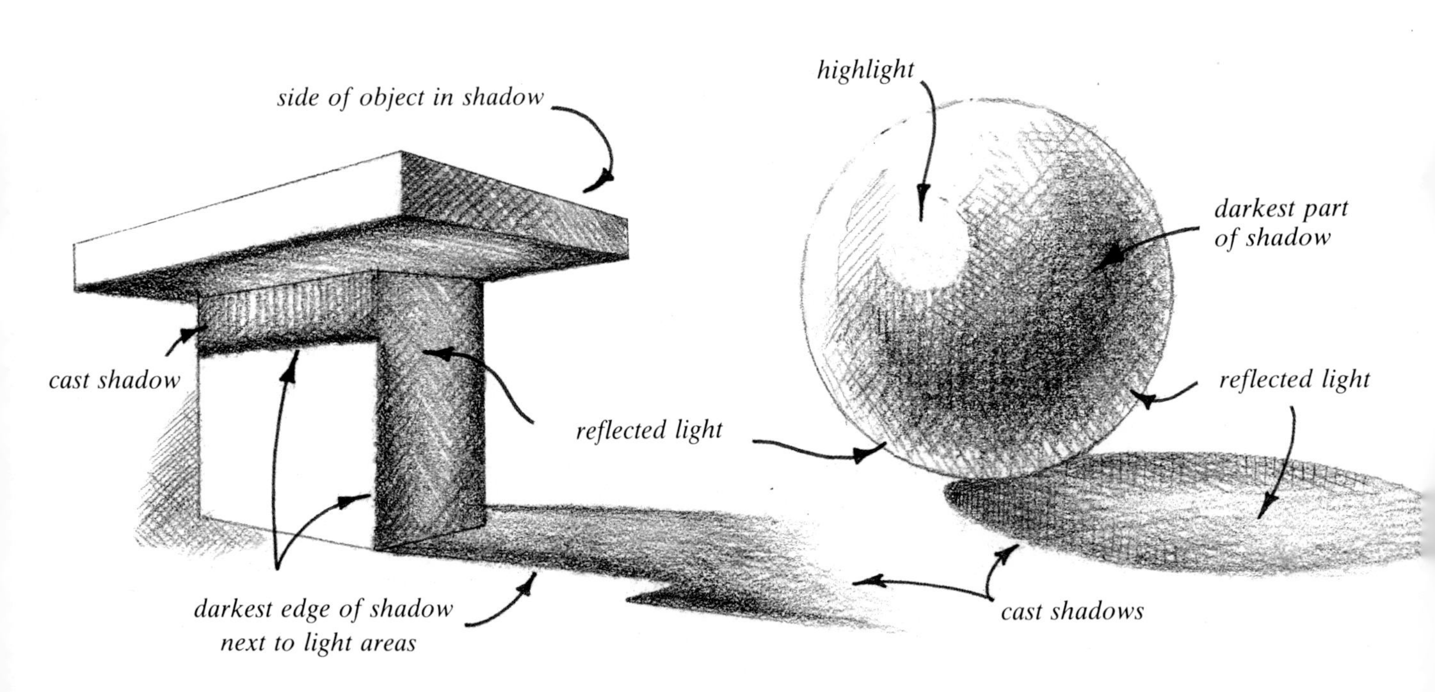

Light and shadow can be suggested, irrespective of what drawing instrument you use – pencils, charcoal, crayons or pen and ink, etc. Cross-hatching, shading and bare white surfaces add form and depth to pictures and shapes.

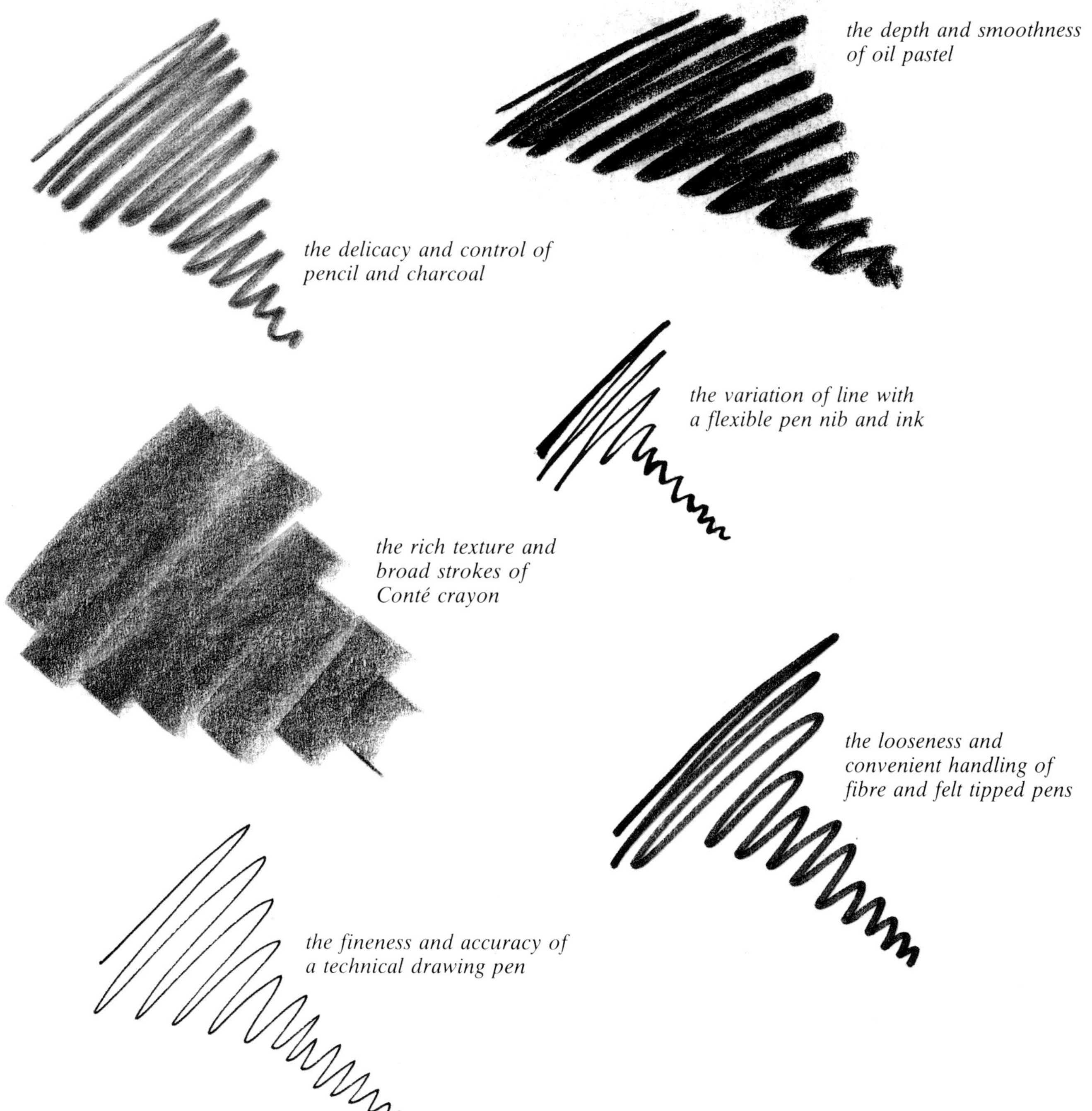

Various marks made by many of the media mentioned in the text.

Pens – ink has a particular quality of its own. When drawing with it, you must decide exactly what you want to do and then do it positively, because pen strokes cannot easily be erased. Special artists' pens give a varied and flexible line according to the pressure used. Cartridge pens are available in a wide variety of nib sizes and are convenient to use because they do not require constant filling.

Fibre and felt tipped pens are easy to use – no sharpening is required! Finished pen sketches can be enhanced by shading with crayon, or by brushing a watercolour wash into certain areas.

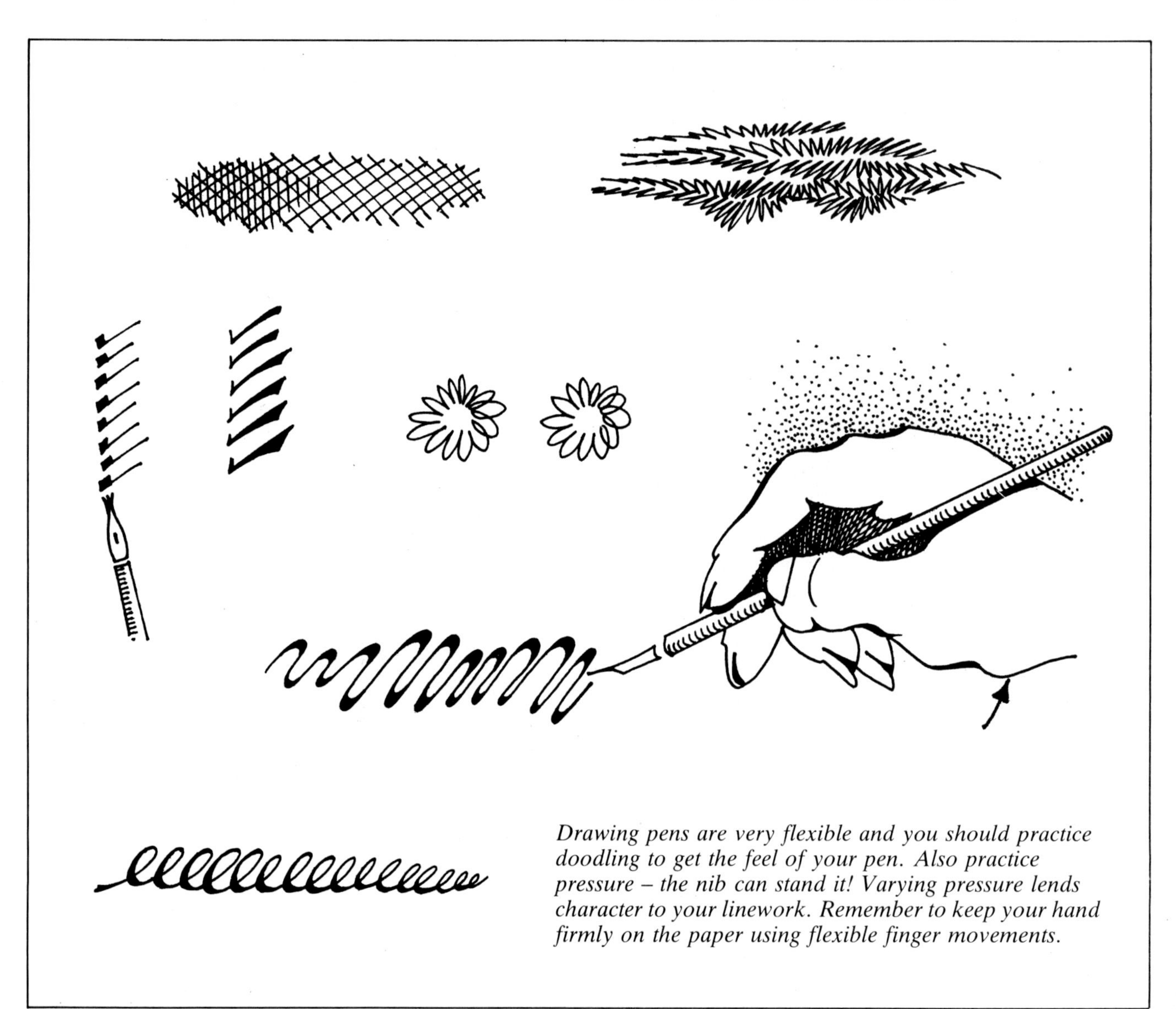

Drawing pens are very flexible and you should practice doodling to get the feel of your pen. Also practice pressure – the nib can stand it! Varying pressure lends character to your linework. Remember to keep your hand firmly on the paper using flexible finger movements.

Starting to draw

It is always wise to spend time studying a subject before starting to draw, and to keep referring to it while transferring your impression on to the paper. As your eye follows the gentle slope of a hillside, the graceful shape of a vase, or the dramatic contours of rocks and falling water, your hand will soon learn to transfer the same shape to the paper almost without you being conscious of the pencil in your hand.

Even when you are working on what you intend to be a highly finished picture, the preliminary sketching-in should be done in this manner, with quick, free lines which pay attention only to essential curves and shading.

The gentle slope of a hillside drawn with a fibre tip pen.

The dramatic contours of rocks and falling water. Fibre tip pen and wash.

A pencil study showing the graceful shape of a vase.

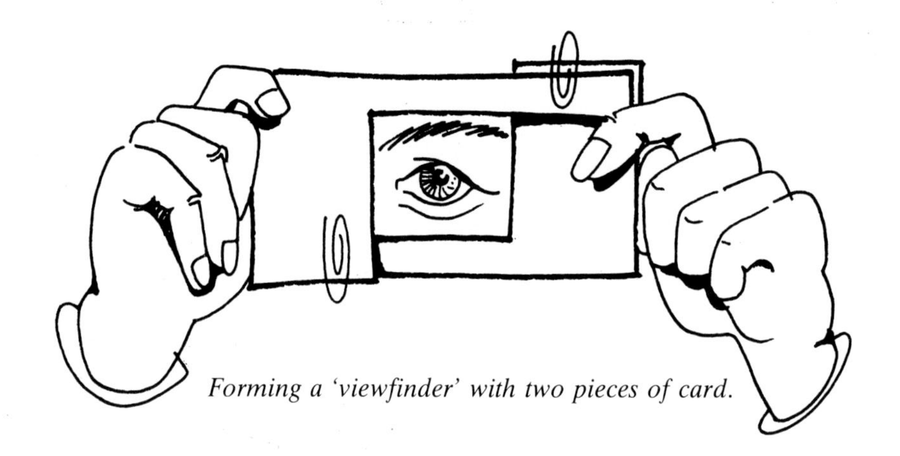

Forming a 'viewfinder' with two pieces of card.

Composition

Careful attention to composition is essential if a picture is to have balance, or a sense of design. Choose an original viewpoint if possible – or at least an angle which shows the subject to its best advantage. For example, if the appeal of an old harbour lies in its being hemmed in by tall cliffs, then avoid making your viewpoint so close up that you have to exclude most of the cliffs; you might find, however, that looking through some foreground rocks or boats will add to the secluded atmosphere.

Some people find a 'viewfinder' useful, (see above). It helps them spot a promising subject. All that is required are two pieces of stiff card with a square or rectangular apperture in the middle, or simply use your hands as shown opposite. This simple construction is helpful in isolating good compositions from a busy scene.

Make up your mind what it is about the subject that appeals to you most and enhance that appeal, even to the exclusion of other attractions. Do not be side-tracked; other subjects can be drawn later on. With a little thought an artist can produce good and original results. We are all individuals and however poor an artist you might think you are, your drawing is an expression of this individuality – even if doing it your own way means breaking the rules!

Pen and ink sketch.

Use your hands to isolate a good composition.
It is a good way of choosing your subject.

Textures

I find the selection of textures illustrated below popping up fairly often in my sketches, irrespective of what I choose to draw with – pencils, pen and ink, crayons or pastels. Practice the art of just 'suggesting' a texture; for example a few slates on a roof area, or a minimum scattering of stones on a beach.

To put the problem simply, where there is an abundance of detail – as in foliage, sky, slates, brick-work, hair, fur, etc. – merely suggest texture by using some of the techniques shown here. The mind's eye is always flexible enough to fill in any extra detail. The examples shown on this page are used throughout the book in a variety of ways.

The importance of light and shade

Make good use of light and shade. Exploit them, even exaggerate them, for they can make an otherwise ordinary drawing into something special. To me, dark shadows and contrasting lighter areas create the magic that transforms a mundane drawing into a picture full of interest and appeal.

When I am drawing, whether it is a small sketch or a highly finished picture, I like to use the same approach. I choose my subject, paying attention to the composition, then study it carefully before working out the perspective, before I transfer my impression to the paper. I show how to build up a drawing in simple stages on page 16, adding texture, light and shadows at each stage.

Contrasting textures are used effectively in this pen and ink drawing of St Michael's Mount, Cornwall. Dark shadows lie against the sunlit terrain adding interest and depth. A detail of the picture opposite is shown above.

Shadows

Having stressed the importance and beauty of shade, I find that the best way of actually drawing shadows using pencils and pens, is with cross-hatching. This technique allows you to overlap lines to create varying degrees of shade and it gives an illusion of depth. Broader drawing tools, such as crayons or brushes, can be used to create

Cross-hatching is an effective way of portraying dark shadows.

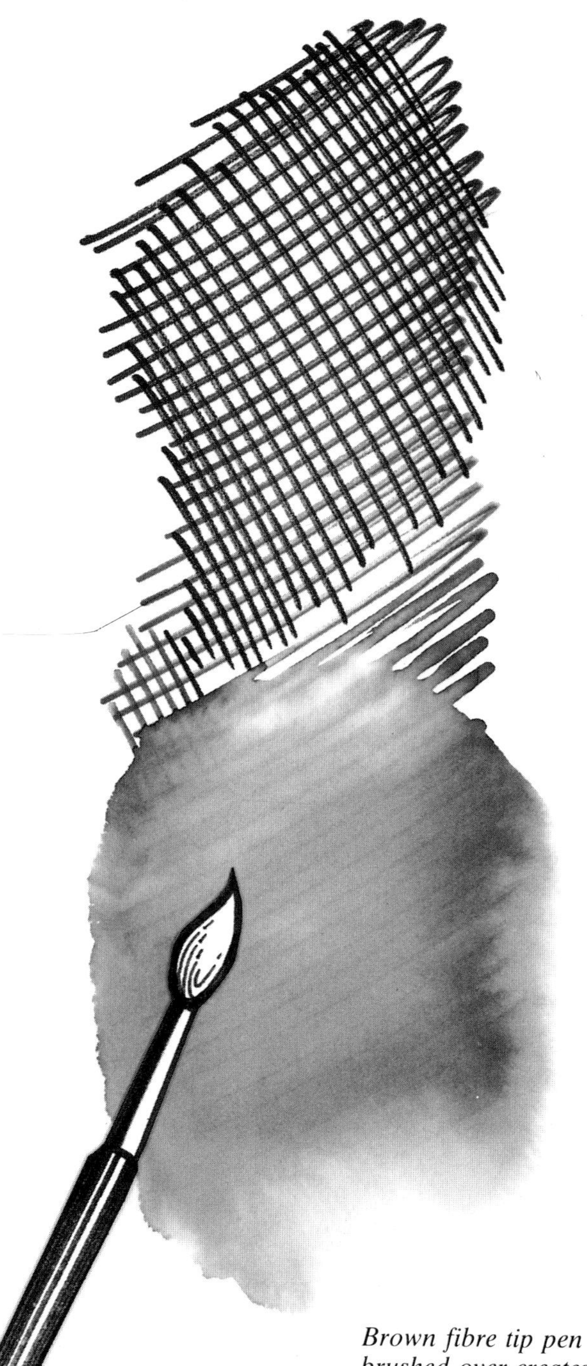

the same effect – shadows and shading are achieved by using broad strokes.

Horizontal, vertical and diagonal strokes can also be used effectively, as can dark areas with very little detail. Contrasting shadows heighten the drama and appeal of a scene.

My observations on light and shade may at first seem to over-complicate what to most people is a simple matter of black and white. But from personal experience I have found it is worth the effort to pay it a little attention. It is a crucial factor in the build-up of a picture.

There are certain points to remember when tackling areas of light and shade and examples of the points listed below are found on the following pages:

1. The lightest lights occur next to the darkest darks.
2. Sunlit areas do not show much texture or detail, whereas shadowed areas show plenty of detail. When drawing in shadows the texture and detail should be combined with plenty of cross-hatching.
3. In bright sunlight the cast shadow is darker than the object in shadow.
4. The shadow cast by an object will follow the contours of the ground or whatever surface the object is standing on. This can offer a variety of dramatic and exciting patterns.

Brown fibre tip pen cross-hatching with a clear wash brushed over creates a lovely warm effect.

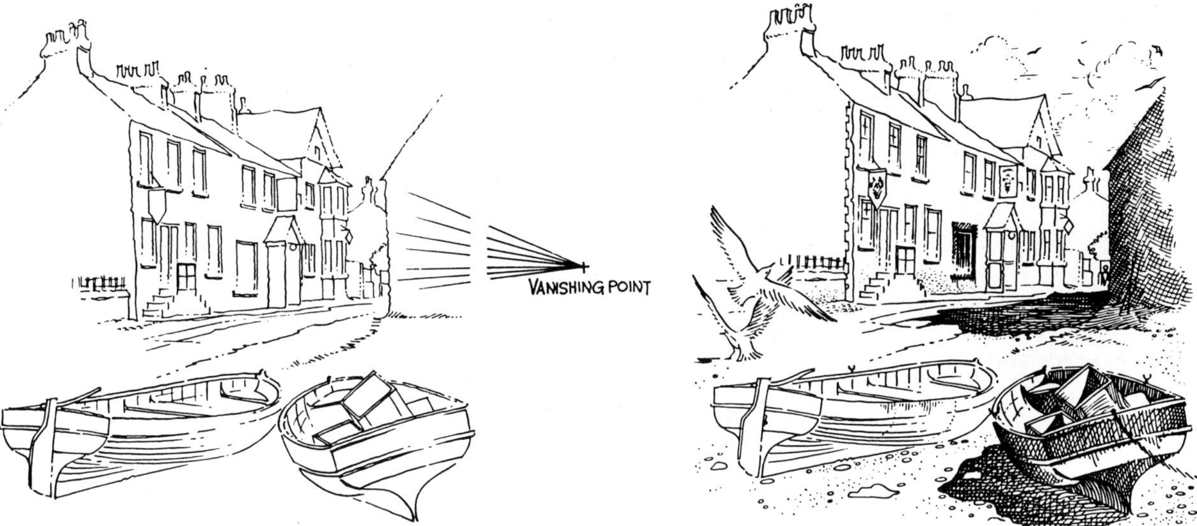

Building up a drawing

The build up to most of my drawings is basically the same. Having chosen my subject, I then work out the perspective.

The first stage is to simply outline the main features, to establish the composition. I then start filling detail, textures and shadows, building up a feeling of light, shade and depth. Finally I keep adding details and shadows until I am satisfied that the drawing is complete.

There is no golden rule which tells you when to stop, except the sooner the better! I like to use a theatrical analogy in this three phase process – build the set; put the props in; then light it!

Using shadows

Good use of shadowing can make or break a picture. Trying to capture the strange shapes cast by one object on to another is a fascinating exercise, and it gives a subject a lovely warmth and atmosphere.

Here, the old motor launch on the canal provides nice reflections. The rippled water breaks the image up into a distorted pattern. Half the picture is thrown into strong silhouette by the sun slanting in from the right. Effective use of straight strokes and some cross-hatching creates the desired effect.

4B pencil sketch.

Strong shadows give a dramatic feel to this pen and ink drawing of a group of cottages.

Many artists tend to look at their chosen subject so full of admiration for it, and with such eagerness to put it down on paper, that they tend to overlook the shadows which sculpture the scene – shadows which form most of its appeal in the first place. The importance of sunlight and shadow cannot be emphasised enough. Indeed, on many occasions I have been tempted to relegate the subject before me to secondary importance, and just to record the wonderful shapes and patterns of the shadows.

'Shadows only' drawings, like the ones here, emphasise the dramatic effects that can be achieved by minimising detail. It is worthwhile for you to try such a study, using different mediums, if only to add experience to the points I have made. If nothing else, you will find it an intriguing exercise. It is surprising how much one can leave out and yet still achieve an excellent result. I sometimes find that the finished drawing is better than a more detailed study would be.

Strong dark shadows are again used here in stark contrast to the glaring white of sunlit buildings. Pen and ink.

Cross-hatching, straight strokes and silhouetting techniques can be combined in a drawing to create atmosphere and heighten a dramatic effect. The drawings here illustrate this beautifully.

The sketch below was initially going to be a preliminary layout for a large oil painting. What fascinated me about the subject was the sun peeping out from behind the tug-boat's smoke, giving the most wonderful 'back-lighting' to the tug and the murky shape of the tanker.

The drawing opposite is a pen and ink study of a fishing village, with pencil shading to add texture and tone. Notice how broad downward strokes illustrate reflected shadows beautifully in the calm isolated puddles of sea water.

4B pencil sketch of a tugboat.

Fishing village in pen and ink, with pencil shading.

Vicarage in pen and ink

Sunlight

Shading, used carefully, can show off sunlight and shadow extremely effectively. I have made a few observations during my studies of this subject, which always help me when I am about to tackle areas of light and shade.

Bright sunlight tends to glare on plain surfaces, thereby cutting down on the amount of textured detail one would normally be able to see. In these highlighted areas, therefore, one should only suggest detail.

Conversely, the shadowed side of an object, a wall for example, shows a lot more detail, plus areas of deeper shade which can be illustrated by cross-hatching.

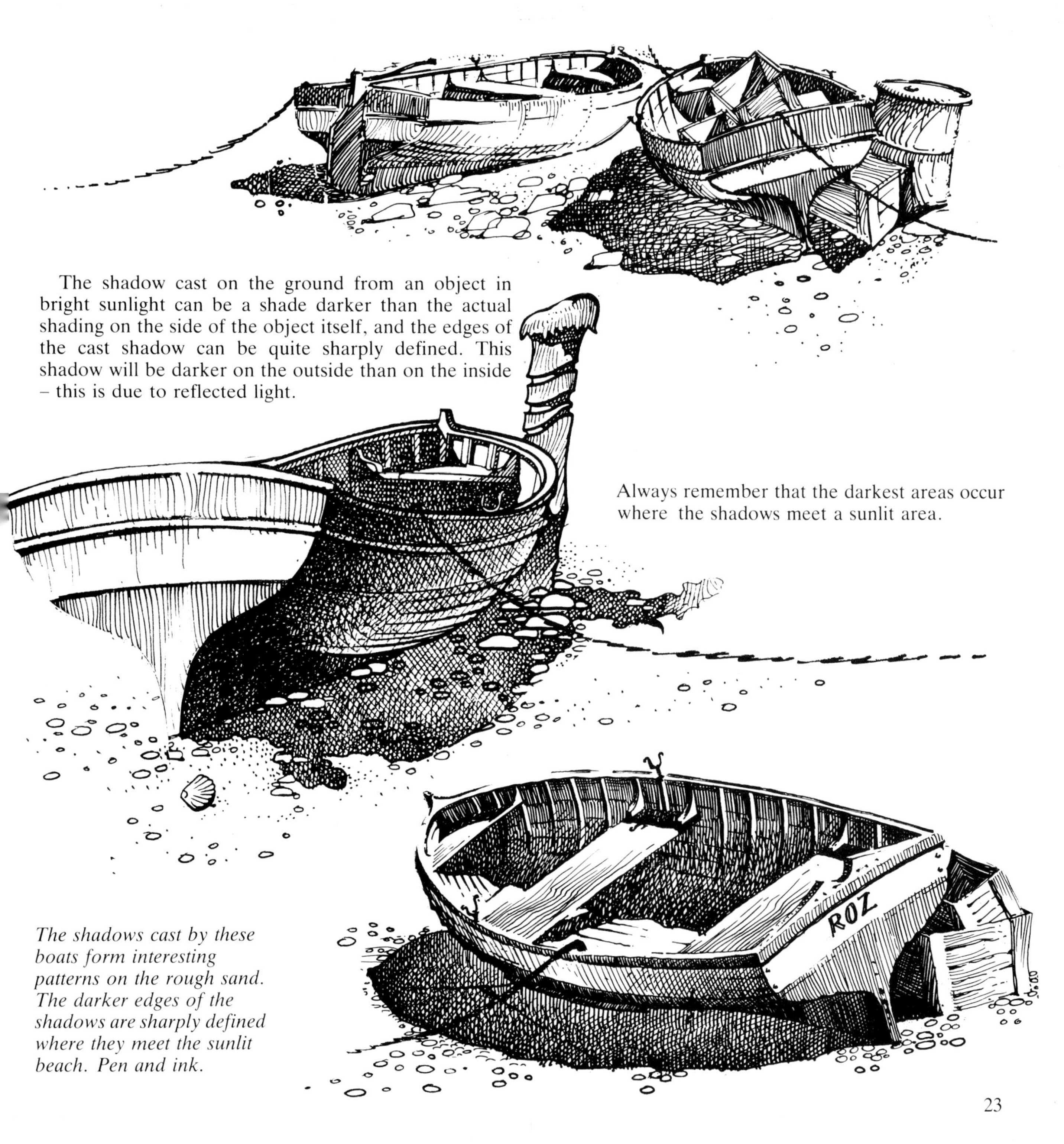

The shadow cast on the ground from an object in bright sunlight can be a shade darker than the actual shading on the side of the object itself, and the edges of the cast shadow can be quite sharply defined. This shadow will be darker on the outside than on the inside – this is due to reflected light.

Always remember that the darkest areas occur where the shadows meet a sunlit area.

The shadows cast by these boats form interesting patterns on the rough sand. The darker edges of the shadows are sharply defined where they meet the sunlit beach. Pen and ink.

The drawings on these two pages illustrate beautifully the contrasts of strong sunlight and dark shadows. They were drawn while I was staying in the Seychelles. The drawing below shows strong areas of light and shade. The sunshine is glaring and the shadows deep and black.

Opposite, the location sketch shows a trading store on the island of Mahé. The store offers a dramatic contrast to the lush vegetation which is bathed in strong sunlight. Strong horizontal strokes vary in tone and merge into deeper recesses and shadows.

Pen and ink sketch showing strong sunlight and shade.

Trading store with felt tip pens in a cartridge paper sketchbook.

Doors and windows

Doors and windows are usually recessed, and you should take advantage of any interesting shadows cast by the reveal or the overhead lintel. Windows, particularly, offer great scope, with shadows and reflected images.

While there is no need to go to any great lengths to reproduce the exact reflection, it does enliven a window if odd, unfinished patterns are drawn on to the glass surface. Glass hardly ever reflects a perfect image, and most reflected images are distorted to a greater or lesser degree.

Country cottage in pen and ink

Opposite: A fibre tip pen and wash of an old timber yard in Interlaken, Switzerland. This drawing exploits the beautiful lighting by looking through the dark, arched interior roof. Doors and windows offer interesting shapes and shadows.

Above: A bay window full of patterns and reflections. Only the frames tie the reflections together and give the sketch shape and form. Pen and ink.

Using the imagination

Above: There is an interesting use of light and shade in this pen and ink study. The viewer's eye is led through the foreground shadows into the sunny churchyard beyond.

There are numerous reasons why some pictures have appeal, while others leave one unmoved. The old maxim is true: 'it's not what you do, it's the way that you do it'.

The most important quality of any sketch or finished picture is its ability to inspire the viewer. For an artist, a drawing talent is not always enough; there is also a need to generate a reaction and a crucial factor to an artist's work is a combination of appeal and response.

There are many pictures which capture my imagination and appeal to me, even though technically they have little merit. Whether by accident or design some artists bring out a response in me and allow me subconsciously to use my imagination. I study their pictures and fill in the gaps in my mind, feel the atmosphere created by the subject, or experience an urgent need to know what is around some mysterious corner. In the drawing opposite I have created an air of mystery with a subtle use of light and shade.

I also find that many perfect examples of an artist's skill leave me cold; having initially admired the professional skill involved in creating the painting or drawing, I quickly become bored. There is little left for my mind to conjure with – no blurred image for me to bring into focus, no obscure shape or shadow for me to peer into. Just as with people, character and individuality generate more interest than an image of perfection with sharp outlines and predictable features.

The lesson to be learnt here is simple in theory, but somewhat more difficult to put into practice. It is not always easy to know where to finish a drawing, or to know how much to put into it or what to leave out. Only practice and experience will teach you this.

Opposite: This pencil drawing epitomises everything I want to convey about light and shade, plus it has a vital air of mystery – there is an urgent need to know what is down the secret passageway. Look at the strokes and cross-hatching, and the texture of the rough stone steps and walls.

Sketchbook studies

I use my sketchbook to record anything I find interesting or unusual; people, places and objects are constant sources of inspiration; shadows, shapes and the interplay and contrasts of light and shade beg to be explored and recorded. I never tire of sketching and enjoy the challenge of putting pen and pencil to paper. It is also useful to have a record of sketches that can be used as reference for future paintings or drawings.

Study of seagulls in 4B pencil.

Jetty in pen and ink.

Lamps in ballpoint pen.

This pencil sketch shows the build up of shadows with cross-hatching. The hairstyle is merely suggested.

Candle in pen and ink.

First published in Great Britain 1989 by Search Press Limited,
Wellwood, North Farm Road, Tunbridge Wells,
Kent TN2 3DR

Reprinted 1997

Text and drawings by Peter Caldwell

ISBN 0 85532 612 3

Distributors to the art trade:

UK
Winsor & Newton,
Whitefriars Avenue, Wealdstone,
Harrow, Middlesex HA3 5RH

USA
Arthur Schwartz & Co.,
234 Meads Mountain Road, Woodstock, NY 12498

New Zealand
Caldwell Wholesale Limited,
Wellington and Auckland

South Africa
Ashley & Radmore (Pty) Limited,
P.O. Box 2794, Johannesburg 2000

Typeset by Scribe Design, 123 Watling Street, Gillingham, Kent Made and printed in Spain by A.G. Elkar S. Coop. Bilbao-12